TRANSCENDING RACE IN AMERICA
BIOGRAPHIES OF BIRACIAL ACHIEVERS

Halle Berry

Beyoncé

David Blaine

Mariah Carey

Frederick Douglass

W. E. B. Du Bois

Salma Hayek

Derek Jeter

Alicia Keys

Soledad O'Brien

Rosa Parks

Prince

Booker T. Washington

PRINCE

Singer-Songwriter, Musician, and Record Producer

David Robson

Mason Crest Publishers

Produced by 21st Century Publishing and Communications, Inc.

MASON CREST PUBLISHERS INC.
370 Reed Road
Broomall, Pennsylvania 19008
(866) MCP-BOOK (toll free)
www.masoncrest.com

Printed in the United States of America.

First Printing

9 8 7 6 5 4 3 2 1

Library of Congress Cataloging-in-Publication Data

Robson, David, 1966–
    Prince : singer-songwriter, musician, and record producer / David Robson.
        p. cm. — (Transcending race in America : biographies of biracial achievers)
    Includes bibliographical references (p.) and index.
    ISBN 978-1-4222-1614-9 (hardback : alk. paper) — ISBN 978-1-4222-1628-6 (pbk. : alk. paper)
    1. Prince—Juvenile literature. 2. Rock musicians—Biography—Juvenile literature. I. Title.
ML3930.P756R63 2010
782.42166092—dc22
[B]   2009022047

Publisher's notes:
All quotations in this book come from original sources, and contain the spelling and grammatical inconsistencies
of the original text.

The Web sites mentioned in this book were active at the time of publication. The publisher is not responsible
for Web sites that have changed their addresses or discontinued operation since the date of publication. The
publisher will review and update the Web site addresses each time the book is reprinted.

Table of Contents

~❁~

" I HAVE BROTHERS, SISTERS, NIECES,
NEPHEWS, UNCLES, AND COUSINS,
OF EVERY RACE AND EVERY HUE,
SCATTERED ACROSS THREE CONTINENTS,
AND FOR AS LONG AS I LIVE,
I WILL NEVER FORGET THAT
IN NO OTHER COUNTRY ON EARTH
IS MY STORY EVEN POSSIBLE. "

" WE MAY HAVE DIFFERENT STORIES,
BUT WE HOLD COMMON HOPES. . . .
WE MAY NOT LOOK THE SAME
AND WE MAY NOT HAVE
COME FROM THE SAME PLACE,
BUT WE ALL WANT TO MOVE
IN THE SAME DIRECTION —
TOWARDS A BETTER FUTURE . . . "

— BARACK OBAMA, 44TH PRESIDENT
OF THE UNITED STATES OF AMERICA

Chapter 1

UPTOWN

ON MARCH 2, 2007, LEGENDARY MUSICIAN and songwriter Prince took the stage for a long-awaited encore. But tonight, he wasn't performing "Kiss," "Pop Life," or one of his many other chart-topping hits. Instead, his peers at the 38th annual NAACP Image Awards were paying tribute to his decades in the music industry.

In a career spanning nearly 30 years, Prince had sold millions of albums and performed his electrifying mix of funk, rock, and jazz for throngs of hungry fans around the world. From his earliest days as a musical **prodigy** playing in the clubs of his native Minneapolis to subsequent music superstardom, Prince defied expectations.

The NAACP Image Awards are a yearly celebration of the achievements made by people of color in television, film, music,

Prince performs in his signature electrifying style during a 2007 concert. His unique approach to music and fashion continues to dazzle eager fans, and the music industry has recognized his outstanding achievements with numerous awards over a career spanning nearly 30 years.

and literature. Notable artists appearing that night at the Shrine Auditorium in Los Angeles included singers Smokey Robinson and Jennifer Hudson, and actors Forest Whitaker and Tyler Perry. But for many music fans, Prince's rare appearance was a highlight.

Prince, who has a reputation for always being fashionably dressed, accepts the 2007 NAACP Image Award for Outstanding Male Artist. In an emotional speech, he touched on the power of music and his desire for artists, rather than businessmen, to control the future direction of music.

NAACP Image Awards: Honor and Controversy

First presented in 1967, the NAACP (National Association for the Advancement of Colored People) Image Awards include 35 categories, including Outstanding Motion Picture and Entertainer of the Year Awards. Over the years, the NAACP Image Awards have grown in status, promoting diversity in the arts. Awards winners include actor Denzel Washington, writer Toni Morrison, and President Barack Obama. But the awards have also attracted controversy. Rapper Tupac Shakur was nominated for an acting award in 1994, despite charges that he abused a woman. At the time, critics argued that Shakur did not present a positive image worthy of award consideration.

STAGE PRESENCE

After being introduced as recipient of the Outstanding Male Artist Award, Prince took the stage. Fashionable as ever, he wore a black and white, Asia-inspired outfit with a high collar. Standing only 5'2", Prince's musical stature was acknowledged with a standing ovation from the crowd.

As he stood behind the podium waiting for the applause to subside, a shy smile spread across his face. Notorious for giving few interviews, the Prince of Pop took a moment to collect his thoughts, raised his hands to quiet the audience, and then spoke. He talked about the eternal power of music and encouraged those in the business side of the industry to let artists control the direction of music in the 21st century:

> **"I would just challenge the phone companies and the new digital providers to allow us . . . to steward the new jazz renaissance, hip-hop, soul [into] the 21st century rather than the accountants and the lawyers who've ruined the music industry."**

Prince's words were hardly a surprise. Even before he sold one record, Prince insisted on controlling his own work. When contracts with record companies limited his ability to release his music, he struck out on his own, devising new methods of reaching his audience. In the 1990s, he even went so far as to change his name in protest for what he considered unfair working conditions. Prince insisted on making music on his own terms.

His years of musical obsession and independence now paid off with an award that some viewed as a capstone to his brilliant career. But at only 48 years old, Prince wasn't slowing down.

LOOKING FORWARD, LOOKING BACK

In the months after receiving his prestigious NAACP award, the Purple One was busier than ever. In July 2007 he released and began promoting a new album, *Planet Earth*. The album cover shows Prince wearing a red shirt—open at the neck—and standing above the blue planet, like a **melodious** sorcerer. Around his neck dangles a gold chain with a pendant combining the symbols for male and female. The title track suggested that the musical wild man of "Let's Go Crazy" had other things on his mind besides partying:

> **"** If planet Earth was in the palm of our hand 50 years
>   from now what will they say about us here?
> Did we care for the fragile water and the atmosphere?
> There's only two kinds of people and the difference
>   they make—
> The ones that give and the ones that take. **""**

The sentiment could also have applied to Prince's foremost obsession: the rules of attraction. His biggest hits charted the often bumpy course of romantic relationships. Songs like "When Doves Cry" and "I Would Die 4 U" spoke of the thrill of being in love. Still, despite what critics often said, Prince did not have a one-track mind. His most highly praised release, 1987's *Sign "☮" the Times* contained blistering social commentary on media culture and the deadly disease AIDS.

Since then, Prince had experienced the high and lows of life and celebrity. He'd suffered personal losses, been involved in exhausting legal disputes, and watched his musical star fade.

On the cover of his 2007 album, *Planet Earth*, Prince seems to be gazing at the world in new ways. While some of his past records featured wild party music, many lyrics on the new album emphasized his concern for the environment and the future of the planet.

But the new millennium also brought with it a greater respect. In 2004, he was inducted into the Rock and Roll Hall of Fame. In the next few years he released half a dozen albums, played at the Super Bowl, and headlined one of the biggest concert tours in music history. While his journey had been long and full of challenges, by 2009 Prince was more relevant than ever.

DELIRIOUS

PRINCE ROGERS NELSON WAS BORN IN Minneapolis, Minnesota, on June 7, 1958. His father, John L. Nelson, played piano in a local jazz combo and went by the stage name Prince Rogers. Prince's mother, the former Mattie Shaw, sang a little and met John when she caught his ears and eyes at an audition.

John was the son of black sharecroppers; his grandparents had been slaves. Yet his family background also included Italian relatives. Mattie considered herself multiracial, often saying that most African Americans had white blood in their lineage. They'd both grown up in the Deep South and moved to Minnesota to escape racism against African Americans. By the time John and Mattie met and married in 1956, the growing family already included children from the couple's previous relationships. John

Prince grew up in Minnesota, where his multiracial family had moved to escape racism in the South. He and his father, a jazz pianist, shared an intense love of music. Both were quiet men and expressed their feelings better through music rather than words.

had a son, John, Jr., and daughters Sharon and Lorna; Mattie had a son, Alfred.

John and Mattie often fought. Prince was 10 when they separated and divorced. At first, Prince lived with his mother, but run-ins with his new stepfather forced him to move to his father's nearby apartment. Father and son were both quiet by nature, but they bonded over music. John later said,

> **❝I express myself through my music and my son does too. That's how we communicate our feelings. A lot of his talent comes from God, maybe some from me.❞**

NEW FAMILY

Music aside, father and son quarreled frequently. The situation came to a head when John kicked Prince out of the house. Luckily, a neighborhood family, the Andersons, took the boy in. Prince already knew the Andersons' son, Andre, and the boys shared a love of music. Their tastes were **eclectic**. Favorites included Earth, Wind & Fire and James Brown.

James Brown: The Godfather of Soul

Born poor in South Carolina in 1933, James Brown's earliest jobs included shining shoes and washing dishes. A natural on the harmonica, guitar, piano, and drums, he dreamed of becoming a performer. Convicted of armed robbery at the age of 16, he began a gospel quartet in prison.

Upon his release Brown joined The Flames, whose 1956 song "Please, Please, Please" sold more than a million copies. A string of hits followed, including "Papa's Got a Brand New Bag" and "I Feel Good." Brown scored a major success when he headlined the Apollo Theater in Harlem in 1963. He commanded the stage, furiously singing and dancing himself into a sweat. Brown's work influenced a generation of singers, including Michael Jackson and Sly & the Family Stone.

Prince and Andre formed a band, Grand Central. They played at local parties and school dances, and their ambitions grew. Bernadette Anderson, Andre's mother, recalls Prince telling her about his post–high school plans:

❝I'm going to get out there and see if I can make it, because if I can't make it in a band I'm coming back here and go to college and major in music.❞

In 1976, Prince recorded a promotional tape. Minneapolis promoter Owen Husney heard the tape, was impressed, and created a marketing campaign to push Prince as an artist of the future. Quickly, Prince was noticed by a variety of major record labels. Offers poured in. But Warner Bros. Records won out.

Prince's early influences included James Brown and Earth Wind & Fire. His amazing musical talent was clear even when he was in high school, and before the age of 20 Prince received recording offers from a number of major labels.

Prince's first album, *For You*, was only moderately successful. His second, self-titled album appeared in 1979, featured two hit singles, and eventually sold more than 1 million copies. When Prince performed a song from the album on TV's American Bandstand, it was clear he was on his way to being a star.

FIRST RECORDINGS

Prince's first official recordings were with the band 94 East, led by Prince's cousin Pepé Willie. But Prince's work writing music for the band was short lived. In 1978, Prince recorded his first album,

For You, playing all 27 instruments on the record himself. It was released two months before his 20th birthday. *For You*, which included the modest hit "Soft and Wet," sold a respectable 430,000 copies in the United States.

For the supporting tour, Prince enlisted a multiracial cast of musicians, including his old friend Andre Anderson (now known as André Cymone). Their first shows, performed at Minneapolis' Capri Theatre, were not a success. Prince mumbled most of his lyrics. His skill on the guitar, though, was undeniable. Inspired in large part by Jimi Hendrix, Prince's blistering axe work made people take notice.

Jimi Hendrix: Guitar Virtuoso

Although he died at 27 in 1970, guitarist Jimi Hendrix is as influential today as ever. Born on a Seattle army base in 1942, Hendrix found an early attraction to the guitar by listening to records and trying to imitate them. After his own stint in the army, Hendrix formed a band with a friend, but the money was bad. He moved to New York City in 1964 and was hired by the Isley Brothers and Little Richard. Hendrix's reputation grew. By 1966, Hendrix had formed his own band, the Jimi Hendrix Experience, with bassist Noel Redding and drummer Mitch Mitchell.

The trio toured Europe and recorded a string of widely praised albums, including *Axis: Bold as Love* and *Are You Experienced*. The Monterey Pop Festival in 1967 made Hendrix big in the United States. His performance at Woodstock in 1969, in which he played an explosive version of "The Star Spangled Banner" made him a legend.

Back in the studio to record *Prince*, the singer regained his confidence. The album yielded two hits, "I Wanna Be Your Lover" and "Why You Wanna Treat Me So Bad" and climbed to number four on the *Billboard* R&B charts. An appearance on the hit dance show American Bandstand in January 1980 was a clear sign that Prince was on his way.

Chapter

3

❧

CONTROVERSY

TWO ALBUMS INTO HIS CONTRACT WITH Warner Bros. Records, Prince had broken through. His work sold well, and his songs were getting radio airplay. Regardless of his potential, Prince was under pressure to produce bigger and bolder albums. *Dirty Mind*, released on October 8, 1980, did the trick.

Critics immediately considered the album a major change from Prince's previous work. The disco-inspired ditties of *Prince* were replaced with punk rock beats and guitar riffs. Prince considered it a truer statement of his musical interests. Side One included the title track, along with the jumpy, **falsetto**-sung "When You Were Mine." Side Two, though, stirred controversy with its explicit language and subject matter. It also included the track "Uptown," Prince's most racially conscious song to date. In it, the speaker imagines a place, referred to as Uptown, where racism and prejudice don't exist:

The 1980s brought a new direction in Prince's music. His album *Dirty Mind* featured punk rock beats and guitar riffs, which listeners found catchy and danceable. His first tour excited new audiences who had never seen Prince dancing and prancing around the stage.

> 66 Now where I come from;
>   We don't let society tell us how it's supposed 2 be.
> Our clothes, our hair, we don't care;
>   It's all about being there.
> Everybody's going Uptown—that's where I wanna be;
>   Uptown—set your mind free. 99

DRESSING THE PART

By 1981, Prince had made a national name for himself. Critics and fans admired his catchy, danceable funk. With his popularity growing and the public anxious to hear the rising star perform live, Prince embarked on his first major tour of the U.S. Now a more confident performer, Prince stoked audiences not only with his music but his onstage antics, which included moving suggestively to the beat.

By now Prince's sense of fashion had also evolved. He began dressing in long coats with bold colors, and took to wearing scarves and makeup. The cover of *Dirty Mind* had featured him in black bikini briefs, a military-style jacket with epaulets, and a bandana tied around his neck. His **androgynous** look fascinated some and disgusted others. Opening for the Rolling Stones at the Los Angeles Coliseum, he was pelted with trash and booed off the stage. Prince, his confidence growing, didn't miss a beat.

Instead, he kept working at a feverish pace. His new album, *Controversy*, reached number 21 on the *Billboard* album chart. Despite his work in fusing different kinds of music, a generation gap persisted when it came to Prince's music. Teenage fans embraced the new, while their parents just didn't get it. Prince later spoke of that disconnect:

> 66 They didn't understand that we are trying to bridge the worlds of rock, funk, jazz and whatever. . . . Older people found it hard to get into us. The kids were the smartest. They're ready for a change. 99

RISING STAR

The song "Controversy" became a hit around the world, and Prince made his first appearance on the late night comedy show *Saturday Night Live.* Even at this early stage of his career, Prince's musical output remained extraordinary. He could spend weeks at a time in the studio recording new songs, pausing only to catch a few hours of sleep and grab a bite to eat.

As usual, he rarely, if ever, used studio musicians, insisting on playing all the parts himself. Prince's output so overwhelmed

Prince worked for weeks nonstop on his 1981 album, *Controversy*. He had a clear vision of the sound he wanted, so he played almost all the musical parts himself, instead of using studio musicians. He created so much new music that the record company couldn't release it fast enough.

Prince was suddenly thrust into the mainstream music spotlight with the release of his 1982 album, *1999*. His new style, the "Minneapolis Sound," launched the record to the top of the charts and helped Prince reach culturally and racially diverse audiences for the first time.

his record company's ability to release his work that he soon hit on a fresh idea: He contacted an old Minneapolis friend, singer Morris Day, and the two worked together on a new album. Prince composed and created all of the music tracks; Day did the singing.

The resulting album, *The Time*, released in 1981, enabled Prince to continue releasing new material without cutting into his official work. It also marked one of the first times that Prince took on a **pseudonym**—the album is credited to producer Jamie Starr. Regardless of who got credit, the new album was a modest hit, reaching number 50 on the *Billboard* album charts.

Morris Day and The Time

Taking inspiration from the 1980 film *The Idolmaker*, Prince created a new band, The Time, as a way of releasing more of his material while promoting the talents of others. The group, which consisted of Morris Day, Jimmy Jam, Terry Lewis, Jellybean Johnson, Monte Moir, Jerome Benton, and Jesse Johnson combined two Minneapolis funk bands, Flyte Time and Enterprise. With Prince's songs, the group scored a number of hits in the 1980s, including "Jungle Love" and "The Bird." But resentment eventually grew between Prince's band members and The Time. Somehow the working relationship continued, with Morris Day taking a star turn in Prince's film *Purple Rain*.

BREAKTHROUGH

Little could have prepared Prince for the acclaim and attention brought on by his next record, *1999*. A double album released in October 1982, it catapulted the 24-year-old Minnesota native to the top of the charts and into the music mainstream.

Combining drum machines and synthesizers, a style dubbed the "Minneapolis Sound," the album climbed onto *Billboard*'s top 10, the first Prince effort to do so. MTV, the new all-music television channel, played the title track video nearly nonstop. But other songs were hits too, including "Delirious" and "Little Red Corvette."

Prince's explosive career marked a cultural **milestone** with *1999*. The subsequent tour, with a new band called The Revolution, also changed perceptions of the singer's music. While his early concerts drew primarily African-American crowds, the *1999* tour grew his audience, according to The Time musician Monte Moir:

> "The *1999* tour was 90 percent black until 'Little Red Corvette' came out. All of a sudden it shifted drastically. It got to be half and half. . . . By the end of the tour, depending on what city, you could see that real crossover was possible."

For an artist intent on reaching across racial and cultural divides, this kind of shift meant everything. It also meant that there was little stopping the man soon to be known as the Purple One.

PURPLE POWER

Prince used his newfound popularity to move in a new direction. As the *1999* tour made its way around the globe, Prince conceived and pitched a film project. The movie, titled *Purple Rain* and shot in Minneapolis, was loosely based on his own rags-to-riches life story. Budgeted at $7 million, Prince starred as "The Kid," a wannabe rock star with a destructive home life. Actress and rumored girlfriend Apollonia Kotero played The Kid's **paramour**, while Morris Day played a rival for her affection.

Naturally, Prince wrote the soundtrack. The first music video from the film, for the song "When Doves Cry," opened with Prince sitting in a steamy bathtub and then crawling naked across the floor. If *1999* made Prince a star, the video and the movie made him an **icon**. Upon its release in the summer of 1984, *Purple Rain* racked up $70 million in ticket sales. The album sold over 13 million copies and spent 24 weeks at number 1 on the charts.

Despite its popularity, the album caused controversy. One song in particular, "Darling Nikki," led Tipper Gore, wife of Senator Al Gore, to begin a campaign to label music. Parents should

The success of the movie and album *Purple Rain* marked a turning point in Prince's career and made him an icon. The title song became a blockbuster. It is one of his signature songs that he still performs at almost every live show.

know, Gore believed, what their children were listening to. Prince's work and Gore's persistence convinced the record industry to voluntarily put Parental Advisory stickers on all records containing explicit material.

NEW DIRECTIONS

Nonstop touring behind *Purple Rain* gave Prince the time to soak up these fresh musical influences and begin work on a new album, which he titled *Around the World in a Day*. The psychedelic sound of songs like "Raspberry Beret" and "Pop Life" owed clear inspiration to certain albums of the 1960s, including *Sgt. Pepper's Lonely Hearts Club Band* by the fab four from Britain, The Beatles.

Initially, Prince refused to do the kind of promotion that had helped *Purple Rain* become such a blockbuster; he resented tabloid reports about his love life and tired of the constant press attention. But under pressure from Warner Bros. he gave in and created music videos for the album, which reached number one but sank quickly out of sight.

He hardly seemed to care. In a few short months Prince was back at Sunset Studios in Los Angeles, firing up a new set of songs and planning a second movie. Recording late into the night and early morning, Prince worked with The Revolution to develop and shape his material. He laid down drum tracks and then built on that foundation with guitar, keyboards, and voices.

He'd given one song, "Kiss," to his **protégés**, a band called Mazarati, but when he heard their version he liked it so much he took the song back. The song appeared on Prince's new album, *Parade*, released in March 1986. Its tight, scratchy beat and sexy lyrics propelled it to the top of the charts. Prince also became the target of criticism. During one interview, a reporter asked him whether he felt he had sold out his black fans by trying to broaden his audience. In response, Prince recalled his listening tastes as a kid:

> **"**I listened to all kinds of music when I was young. . . . I always said that one day I would play all kinds of music and not be judged for the color of my skin but the quality of my work, and hopefully I will continue.**"**

STUMBLES AND SUCCESS

Although *Parade* became a modest hit, Prince's second shot at silver screen stardom, *Under the Cherry Moon*, was troubled from the beginning. Filmed on location in Italy and shot in black and white, the romantic comedy's director, Mary Lambert, was fired over creative differences after only four days. Prince took over, but he had little experience managing a Hollywood movie set. The onscreen results received mixed reviews at best and bombed at the box office.

Prince directed himself in this scene from his second film, *Under the Cherry Moon*, which was a box-office flop. He faced other difficulties when his band fell apart and he constantly disagreed with his record company. Finally, though, he had chart-topping success with his 1987 album, *Sign "☮"the Times*.

Prince's dream of his own recording studio became a reality in 1987, when he opened Paisley Park near Minneapolis. He soon recorded two albums but only released the second, *Lovesexy*. Although he toured with a new band, neither the supporting tour nor the album were big moneymakers.

Prince retreated to Minneapolis where he built a new home in Chanhassen, Minnesota, and went forward with plans to construct a state-of-the-art studio nearby. Then, in the spring of 1986, Prince's band, The Revolution, revolted. Band members Wendy and Lisa, especially, were dumbfounded when Prince added new members to the already tight group. Soon after, The Revolution fell apart completely when Prince fired Wendy, Lisa, drummer Bobby Z. Rivkin, and bassist Mark Brown.

More work became Prince's **mantra**. In a flurry of activity, he recorded three albums, abandoning them all and then refashioning the material into *Crystal Ball*. Prince's vision included a package containing three LPs (long playing albums). Warner Bros. refused to release the material, believing they'd make little profit from such an unusual project.

For the first time in his career, Prince argued fiercely with the record company. In the end, though, he agreed to a two-disc album that he retitled *Sign "☮" the Times*. Appearing in March 1987, the record received fantastic reviews—the best of his career—and snaked slowly but steadily up the charts. Hits included "U Got the Look," "I Could Never Take the Place of Your Man," and the socially relevant title track.

NEW STUDIO AND NEW MUSIC

In 1987, Prince's dream of a studio to call his own came true with the opening of Paisley Park, near Minneapolis. Envisioned as a music and movie-producing factory, its 55,000 square feet of office and studio space allowed the superstar a creative playhouse to call his own. Warner Bros. helped fund the facility.

He recorded *The Black Album* in late 1987. But despite it being hailed by Prince as the "Funk Bible," he withdrew the work only days before its release. Reasons remain unclear, but theories circulated: Prince came to consider the work evil, or Prince and Warner Bros. deemed the work too suggestive and dark. While neither of these reasons has been confirmed, Prince quickly tried to redeem himself.

Prince returned to the limelight with his successful soundtrack to the movie *Batman*. However, his own movie, *Graffiti Bridge*, wasn't as well received. Audiences found his directorial and starring roles dull and lifeless, and suddenly his popularity was on the skids again.

He spent eight weeks recording *Lovesexy*, which included the song "Alphabet St." Prince viewed the record as more positive than *The Black Album*, yet sales fell flat. The supporting tour with his new unnamed band included 84 shows and was well received critically, but it lost money in the end.

BATMAN AND GRAFFITI

Prince had two new projects in the works by early 1989, but he was convinced to put them on hold by film director Tim Burton. *Batman*, a movie version of the comic book superhero, was slated for a June release, and Burton thought Prince the perfect performer to spice up the soundtrack. But while Burton only asked for two or three songs, Prince produced a nine-track album. *Batman*, the movie soundtrack, sold nearly five million copies and made Prince relevant again.

Caped Crusaders: Prince and Batman

By the summer of 1989, Warner Bros. was looking for a project to catapult Prince back into the limelight. Between February and March, Prince recorded tracks to accompany the most hotly anticipated movie of the year. Director Tim Burton had built a reputation for weird, quirky films starting with *Pee Wee's Big Adventure* and *Edward Scissorhands*. Now, he needed music to complement his images of a mysterious hero and his **nemesis**, the clown-faced Joker. Prince reworked three tracks he'd recorded the previous year. To tie the film and music more closely together, Prince sampled dialogue from the movie. As part of his deal, Prince agreed to surrender the rights to the songs on the *Batman* soundtrack. Thus, none of the tracks appear on any greatest hits album.

Yet after a 1990 tour, Prince baffled his fans again, with the movie *Graffiti Bridge*. As with his prior film work, Prince starred. He also directed again. In an attempt to recapture the glory of *Purple Rain*, Prince played the Kid, with Morris Day once again playing his rival. Filmed at Paisley Park, the movie appeared lifeless on screen. Audiences stayed away in droves, making it Prince's biggest failure to date. While the soundtrack album fared better, producing the hit "Thieves in the Temple," music's former golden child watched as his popularity fell into steep decline.

Chapter

4

POP LIFE

THE PRINCE OF 1991 FOUND HIMSELF IN a transformed musical landscape. A tuneful tidal wave known as **Grunge** had crashed down upon the music industry. Groups like Nirvana, Pearl Jam, and Alice in Chains tapped into a new vein of teen **angst** and brought the new music into the mainstream of American popular music.

Nearly 13 years after his debut album, Prince continued defying musical trends. By 1991, he also had a new band: The New Power Generation (NPG). Gone were the drum machines of the past. Instead, many of the latest songs were recorded live in the studio with the entire band.

The first official album credited to the newfangled band, *Diamonds and Pearls*, featured a holographic cover picturing Prince and two new dancers, Lori Werner and Robia LaMorte. The women, nicknamed Diamond and Pearl, also appeared in videos

Prince had new hope and a freshly formed band in 1991, as he recognized the changing directions in which music was headed. He brought out the album *Diamonds and Pearls*, featuring two new dancers who appeared in his music videos and helped make the album a smash hit.

Pop superstar Michael Jackson performs at the 1995 MTV Video Music Awards. As Michael was signing a long-term record deal, Prince was negotiating his own contract with Warner Bros. But the deal was controversial, and both sides disagreed on terms, setting themselves up for future conflicts.

for the album. These beauties swirling to the beat of Prince's pop did the trick with fans. The album was a smash. But some critics, like the *New York Times* critic Jon Pareles, saw the work as Prince's desperate effort to keep up with the changing times:

> **"Prince has become an outsider. He has been blind-sided by hip-hop; the rise of rap suddenly made him feel old-fashioned. . . . *Diamonds and Pearls* suggests he has figured out a survival strategy: keep his ears open, keep dancing and leering, and hide his hybrids behind the trends."**

If *Diamonds and Pearls* kept dancing near the top of the charts, his attention was also being pulled in other directions. More artists were covering his songs. In 1991, he provided new songs to Céline Dion and Joe Cocker. He also began work on a short film for his latest girlfriend and future wife, Mayte Garcia.

NEW DEAL, NEW PROBLEMS

In 1991, a number of performers signed **lucrative**, long-term contracts, including King of Pop Michael Jackson, who inked a six-album, $60 million deal with Sony. Prince knew that his brand —the reputation he had earned over the years—remained strong.

Music and Money

Before the advent of iTunes and mp3s, record companies and artists made most of their money by selling albums and singles. Yet many of the pioneering music-makers of the 20th century received little or no financial reward for their work. The Blues, the basis of much of modern rock and roll, produced the likes of Muddy Waters, Howlin' Wolf, and Willie Dixon.

But when the songs of these artists were covered by British and American rock and rollers like Elvis Presley, Eric Clapto[n], The Rolling Stones, little credit or [...] made its way back to the originator[s]. *Zeppelin II*, released in 1969, came u[p] review when it became clear that a nu[mber] of songs on the British band's album [...] based on the work of bluesmen Willie D[ixon] and Sonny Boy Williamson. Law[suits] followed, with the legal tangle event[ually] leading to songwriting credit and pa[y for] their efforts.

Warner Bros. loved what Prince had done for their record company. His enormous success in the 1980s and with *Diamonds and Pearls* suggested that his career would continue blossoming. Still, Prince's work could be erratic, and, at times, a bit strange.

Negotiations over a new contract began in the summer of 1992. The two sides hammered out a new, six-record contract worth $100 million in late August 1992. From the start, the contract was controversial. Prince's representatives bragged about the deal, which at first glance seemed larger than other recent contracts. Many in the industry were baffled, since Prince's record sales never approached those of Michael Jackson or Madonna.

Warner Bros. felt that Prince and his people misrepresented the true nature of the deal they'd agreed to. A growing resentment between the two parties developed which, over time, would threaten Prince's very career.

THE SYMBOL

The first release under the new deal posed immediate problems, beginning with the title. The **hieroglyph** Prince chose to serve as the title was unpronounceable. It appeared to fuse the ancient symbols of male and female, but the artist himself provided no real explanation. Warner executives believed that trying to market an album with such an obscure title might pose a challenge and hurt its sales.

Warner Bros. also disagreed with Prince over which single to release first. Prince insisted on "My Name is Prince" because he thought it sounded similar to the songs on *Diamonds and Pearls*. Warner pushed for the track "7," which they felt had more hit potential. Prince wouldn't budge, later saying,

> **"What I was doing wasn't about arrogance, it was about someone trying to put me in a paper cage, and tell me, a grown man, what I couldn't do."**

After heated exchanges, Warner finally gave in. Upon its release, "My Name is Prince" stalled at number 36 on the *Billboard* Hot 100

Prince decided on a "glyph" as the title of his 1992 album, which came to be known as *The Love Symbol*. This didn't sit well with record company executives, but even more friction was created when Prince changed his name to that unpronounceable symbol.

chart. The other single, "7," fared better, reaching number 7. Overall the album, Prince's second with The New Power Generation, sold nearly 3 million copies. Still, both Prince and Warner Bros. considered it a disappointment.

BAD BLOOD

The bad blood between Prince and Warner Bros. reached a climax when Prince made a dramatic decision: he changed his name from Prince to the unpronounceable glyph he'd used on his last album.

Prince still created magic with his guitar, but 1990s critics said he was releasing too many lackluster albums too quickly. His name change and erratic behavior didn't help matters, and some people feared for his mental health and the future of his career.

Angry at what he perceived as a poor promotion campaign for his previous record and for other slights, he decided to go into the studio, work at a furious pace, and produce the final albums he owed Warner Bros. under his contract.

Stage Names

While Prince is not the only musician to ever change his name, he may be one of the first to do so in the midst of a successful career. Prince contemporary Madonna kept her first name, but dropped her last, Ciccone, long before she hit the big time. Rapper T-Pain, searching for street cred, retired Faheem Najm. Other artists take on fake names, or pseudonyms, as a way of dropping their musical baggage. In the mid-1980s, well-known singer and songwriter Elvis Costello recorded for a while as Napoleon Dynamite; former Beatle Paul McCartney attempts to escape his legend from time to time when he records as The Firemen with record producer Youth.

For their part, record company staff became disenchanted with a man once considered their greatest hit-maker. According to one Warner employee, Marylou Badeaux, few could take it anymore:

"The mood was that people had had it. People were saying to me, 'This guy is out of control.'"

The record company's other concern was the frequency with which Prince, now being called "The Artist Formerly Known as Prince," put out new records. One reason The Artist's albums were not selling so well, they suspected, was that there were so many of them being released too quickly.

But in 1994, The Artist convinced them to put out another, titled *Come.* Selling less than 500,000 copies, it only served to reinforce the record company's concerns. *The Gold Experience*, his next release, fared far better and contained the hit single "The Most Beautiful Girl in the World." Many fans saw it as their idol's best work of the 1990s. But The Artist continued to be ridiculed in the press for his name change, with some critics suggesting he was killing his career on purpose.

In the late 1990s, The Artist Formerly Known as Prince realized that his songwriting was still excellent, but that quality did not necessarily sell pop hits. So he worked hard to promote his own albums and was one of the first to recognize the power of the Internet to increase record sales.

Weirdness continued, as The Artist, in interviews, spoke of "Prince" as if he were another person:

> **Prince never used to do interviews. You'd have to ask Prince why he never used to do interviews, but you're not talking to Prince now, you're talking to me.**

Close associates worried about his mental health, but The Artist continued working to finish his Warner Bros. contract, often using older material to fill out a CD.

LAST AND FIRST

The Artist's last album under his contract came out in 1996. Its title, *Chaos and Disorder*, seemed to reflect the **dysfunctional** relationship he had with Warner Bros.

But if the former Prince's career appeared to be in freefall, his personal life seemed to be deepening. On Valentine's Day 1996, he married longtime girlfriend Mayte Garcia. In October, Mayte gave birth to a baby that the couple named Boy Gregory. Tragically, after only seven days, the child died from a genetic disorder.

Around this time, The Artist also began exploring the Jehovah's Witnesses religion. Musically, he attempted a comeback. He released a triple album, *Emancipation*, in late 1996 through his own label, NPG Records. Few fans seemed to care. The Artist said in an interview in 1997 that his songwriting had not changed; he also implied that quality and commercial success do not always go together:

> **"Radio, video and media dictate what is a 'hit.' I still, and always have, written the same. Only now there may possibly be a bit more truth to my work. As the soul grows, so does the message."**

Still, he did try to sell his work, now using the Internet. While The Artist's efforts initially yielded mixed results, he was one of the first to recognize the power of the Web to promote music.

Like his career, The Artist's personal life was going sour. After nearly 10 years together, the former Prince and Mayte divorced. As usual, he worked through personal pain by making music. His last album of the 1990s, *Rave Un2 the Joy Fantastic* was released but it, too, failed commercially.

On December 31, 1999, the pay-per-view special *Rave Un2 the Year 2000* debuted. Featuring a concert recorded two weeks earlier, live versions of "Purple Rain" and "1999" reminded viewers of the power and artistry of a man who now stood at a crossroads: Could the artist once known as Prince reinvent himself one more time, or would these performances serve as the closing chapter to a once stellar career?

SIGN "" THE TIMES

WITH THE 1990S OVER, THE ARTIST FORMERLY Known as Prince tried to look forward. He had little choice: poor album sales and dwindling fan support forced him to rethink his career. A first step on the long road to rock and roll recovery was taken on May 16, 2000.

At a press conference, he announced another name change. This time, though, people would have no trouble pronouncing it. The former Prince became Prince once again, reclaiming his birthright as well as his reputation.

Prince also retooled his Web site. Fans could catch up with their idol by subscribing to the service on a monthly basis or for a lifetime. Prince envisioned NPGMusicClub.com as a way of reaching out to fans by providing them access to concert sound checks and yearly celebrations at Paisley Park Studios.

Prince greeted the new millennium by taking back his original name, reworking his Web site, and trying new experiments to get his career back on track. While record sales fluctuated, critics continued to respect his unique music and otherworldly approach to stardom.

NEW DIRECTION

Musically, the early years of the new decade found Prince in an experimental mood. In 2001, *Rainbow Children*, the first album released through the new Web site, featured songs about love but also focused heavily on social change.

For the most part, fans did not embrace this jazzier album, yet Prince continued following his own musical **muse** and earning the respect of others. Senior editor of *Esquire* magazine Wendell Brown noted Prince's uniqueness:

66 **Prince is one of the few celebrities that truly marches to the beat of his own drum. . . . He is a true reflection of his music, larger than life, outrageous and absolutely not rooted in any familiar trends. He is otherworldly.** 99

As for his personal muse, her name was Manuela Testolini, a raven-haired Canadian beauty who'd met Prince at Paisley Park, where she worked for one of his charitable foundations. After a brief courtship, the two married in Hawaii on New Year's Eve 2001.

RELOADED

Prince remained persistent and **prolific**. He released the quiet, voice and piano work *One Nite Alone*, which included a cover of a Joni Mitchell song, "A Case of U." He followed up with his first live album, *One Nite Alone . . . Live!*

Before long, though, Prince turned up the volume once again. In early 2004, he was invited to perform at the Grammy Awards. Dressed in a dark suit and bathed in purple lights, Prince descended a staircase holding his glyph-shaped guitar. As the crowd went wild, he sang the first few bars of "Purple Rain." He looked confident and commanding.

At the end of the first chorus, songstress Beyoncé Knowles joined in, with Prince adding sharp guitar licks. The pair continued the medley with "1999," "Baby I'm a Star," "Let's Go Crazy," Beyoncé's "Crazy in Love," and finished with a Prince guitar solo.

One month after his widely praised Grammy performance, Prince was inducted into the Rock and Roll Hall of Fame in Cleveland, Ohio. Introduced by Alicia Keys and members of the hip hop duo OutKast, Prince later joined the musical tribute to fellow inductee the late George Harrison by contributing a guitar solo to the Harrison tune "While My Guitar Gently Weeps." Like former Beatle Harrison, the quality of Prince's songs inspired other singers to cover them on their own records.

Prince released *Musicology* in April 2004. The concert tour that followed provided a unique twist: each fan who purchased a ticket to a show received a copy of *Musicology*. The record quickly became his biggest hit since *Diamonds and Pearls* more than a decade earlier. The tour earned $87.4 million, the highest earning of the year; his powerhouse performances got rave reviews.

Prince and Beyoncé go all out at the 2004 Grammy Awards. Their electrifying performance of a number of his hits, and Prince's electrifying guitar solo, gained rave reviews from critics and fans. That year Prince was also honored for his songwriting with his induction into the Rock and Roll Hall of Fame.

Prince was not always a fashion leader. Originally dressing for shock value, he has now become a style icon. For many years his clothes were mainly purple, but now his suits are more quietly fashionable. Prince's wardrobe is one of the most unique and creative in the music business.

Covering Classics: The Music of Prince

One sign of a songwriter's influence and longevity is how often his work is performed by other artists. Judged by this criterion, Prince's music will live on for generations. Before most people even knew he wrote it, singer Chaka Khan turned Prince's "I Feel for You" into a hit in 1984. Mariah Carey included a version of "The Beautiful Ones" on her 1997 smash album *Butterfly*.

Dozens of acts have paid Prince the highest compliment by recording his songs. In 1990, Irish songstress Sinéad O'Connor recorded a Prince-penned song that he had never sung himself, "Nothing Compares to You." O'Connor's version became an immediate number one smash hit, earning her three Grammy nominations and one award, for Best Alternative Music Performance.

Now, Prince's music took center stage, not sexy dancers or raunchy lyrics. For the first time, his religious beliefs also found a home on stage. During "Purple Rain," Prince even told concert-goers to read their Bibles, aware that as a **journeyman** artist, people of all ages now attended his shows. He spoke of the changes:

"I have a responsibility to the children that come to my concerts to not to expose them to anything that would be, you know, considered raunchy [or] risqué. I'm not trying to be obscene to anybody."

Clothes Horse: The Style of Prince

He began his careering by shocking people. Dressed in black bikini briefs and shaking his booty, Prince evolved over the years into one of the more stylish music superstars. In the early days he sported ruffled shirts and long, colorful coats. By the time of *Purple Rain*, the royal color accented with white lace had become his trademark.

As Prince matured, custom-made suits by the likes of designers Alexander McQueen, Burberry, and Roberto Cavalli became the norm. He often tops off his wardrobe with a stylish derby hat. On stage, he dresses for comfort and may don a doo-rag to match his shiny lizard-like suit and coral-inspired necklace. At the 2007 NCLR Alma Awards, the artist stood out in all white. Small but long-limbed, Prince's sophisticated and dazzling attire makes him the center of attention wherever he appears.

Prince accepts the award for Best Male R&B Artist during the 2006 BET Awards. That night marked new career beginnings for the artist, as he sang with superstars Chaka Khan and Stevie Wonder and later performed singles from his recent hit album, *3121*.

REWARDS AND CHARITY

The 2004 Prince **juggernaut** continued when *Musicology* received two Grammy awards. *Rolling Stone* magazine also released its list of the "100 Greatest Artists of All Time," with Prince landing at number 28.

In the aftermath of 2005's Hurricane Katrina, which devastated Louisiana and Mississippi, Prince quickly recorded a new song, "S.S.T.," and posted it for downloading on his Web site and on iTunes.

Inspired by the Sade song "The Sweetest Taboo," the **acronym** of the title also stood for the term "Sea Surface Temperature," a reference to the way scientists track hurricanes. The song quickly rocketed to number one on the iTunes R&B charts. Prince generously donated all proceeds from the song to helping victims of the disaster.

PRINCE MATTERS

On March 21, 2006, he released *3121*. It debuted atop the *Billboard* album charts, the first Prince album to ever do so. Critics and fans alike viewed the work as part of a rebirth for the funk **maestro**. According to *Rolling Stone* critic Brian Orloff, Prince's return to form was welcome:

> **"Though his songs might be slightly more PG-13 these days, Prince still injected some much-needed adult content into a chart recently dominated by the underage set."**

In June, television viewers got a close look at the star when he appeared at the annual BET Awards in Los Angeles, which recognize the year's best African-American entertainers. The night's stars included Beyoncé, Jay-Z, 50 Cent, and Lil Wayne. Early in the evening, Prince picked up an award for Best Male R&B Artist. Looking surprised as he mounted the stage, the veteran performer told the audience how good it felt to be back. But the award was only the beginning of Prince's big night.

Soon after, he hit the stage with fellow legends Stevie Wonder and Chaka Khan. The three teamed on a roaring version of Prince's "I Feel for You," in honor of Chaka Khan's Lifetime Achievement Award. It was the first time Prince and Chaka had sung the hit together. Later, Prince completed his musical hat trick by performing pieces from *3121*, which continued its perch near the top of the charts.

BIG STAGE

Prince performed for his largest audience ever when he played the halftime show at Super Bowl XLI on February 2, 2007. With nearly 150 million people tuning in around the world, Prince raced through shortened versions of "Let's Go Crazy" and "Baby I'm a Star," as well as snatches of Queen's "We Will Rock You" and Bob Dylan's "All Along the Watchtower." The capacity crowd at Dolphin Stadium in Miami exploded.

The day after show, critics were citing the wild, purple-lit extravaganza as the best Super Bowl performance ever. Yet not all viewers were pleased. Some in the media criticized one aspect of the performance: During his rendition of "Purple Rain," Prince stood behind a large beige curtain with only his silhouette visible. While a few thought the image too suggestive, others dismissed the claims as silly. Suggestive or not, this was Prince, after all, a man who had always enjoyed pushing boundaries.

His NAACP Image Award for Outstanding Male Artist presented one month later further proved his staying power. But Prince couldn't stay long. He was again on the move. This time, he'd set dates for an unprecedented series of concerts.

In the early days of his career, Europe had taken a while to embrace Purple Power. Now, Prince stood on top of the music world. He would perform seven concerts at London's O2 Arena, one of Europe's largest indoor concert venues. The tickets sold out in 20 minutes, so he added 8 more shows for a total of 15.

For any act to fill 20,000 seats for two straight weeks seemed like pure fantasy. But during his long career, Prince had often made a habit of turning fantasy into reality. The tickets were again snapped up. Ticket demand remained so overwhelming that Prince added 6 more shows, for a total of 21. The book *21 Nights*, written by Prince and photographer Randee St. Nicholas, chronicles the whirlwind of Prince in London.

Prince performs for his largest audience ever during half-time at Super Bowl XLI in 2007. The wildly cheering crowd and critics agreed that the event was the best Super Bowl performance they had ever seen. Soon after, Prince toured Europe and triumphantly filled a 20,000-seat venue for 21 performances.

Prince closes the show in style at the 2008 Coachella Music and Arts Festival. His virtuoso performance reminded audiences that Prince's future is still bright after almost 30 years on the music scene. But Prince prefers to focus on the present, and the joy that music brings him and his fans every day.

THE SHOW THAT NEVER ENDS

A year later, in April 2008, Prince headlined the ninth annual Coachella Festival in Indio, California. The three-day event included dozens of alternative acts performing on a variety of stages.

Prince signed on for the gig three weeks before it opened, but some in the audience still wondered whether he even fit the definition of "alternative" in the first place. Judging by his musical superstardom, he seemed the epitome of mainstream, especially when compared to other artists on the bill like Portishead and Sri Lankan singer M.I.A.

For festival organizers, Prince's inclusion may simply have been a way to sell more tickets. But once he took the stage, he offered the crowd a lesson in musical credibility. For two hours, Prince whipped through a selection of his hit songs and threw in a couple of covers, including Radiohead's "Creep," for good measure. At one point, during his song "Shhh," he held a single guitar note for 25 seconds before plowing ahead. At the end of his blistering set, few could argue with his virtuoso performance.

FLOWER POWER

His next record, titled *Lotusflow3r*, continued the innovations Prince was known for. In an exclusive deal with Target stores, the package released on March 29, 2009, and contained three CDs: *Lotusflow3r*, *Mplsound*, and the debut work of Prince's protégé, Bria Valente. Priced at $11.98, the collection was considered a bargain by both critics and fans.

After 31 years, hundreds of awards, and millions of albums sold, Prince headed into the future more beloved and popular than ever. But he wasn't looking ahead. Instead, he spoke of living in the present, making new music, and continuing his journey as one of music's most legendary performers:

> **"I don't think about the future. I have to make the music I have to make now, and I have to go where the spirit takes me . . . and because I approach things like that, I enjoy every day so much more."**

1958   Prince Rogers Nelson is born on June 7 in Minneapolis, Minnesota.

1975   Prince graduates high school a year early, after having formed the 12-member band Grand Central in junior high.

1977   At 19, Prince signs a $1 million contract with Warner Bros. Records.

1978   Prince releases his debut album, *For You*. He produces the album, plays all the instruments, and sings all the vocals. Critics praise the effort, but sales are modest.

1979   After signing with the Cavallo/Ruffalo and Fargnoli management agency, Prince's second effort, *Prince*, is certified platinum (1 million copies sold).

1980   *Dirty Mind* is released to great controversy for its explicit lyrics.

1981   Prince's new album, *Controversy*, sells one million copies in the United States; as an opening act for the Rolling Stones in Los Angeles, he is booed off the stage.

1982   The double-album *1999* sells 3 million copies, becoming Prince's biggest hit to date. For the second year in a row, he is voted Musician of the Year at the Minnesota Music Awards.

1983   Prince wins six awards at the Minnesota Music Awards and begins filming his first movie, "Purple Rain," in Minneapolis.

1984   *Purple Rain* is released, along with a soundtrack by Prince. The soundtrack sells 11 million copies; the film grosses $70 million at the box office.

1985   Prince starts his own record label, Paisley Park, and releases *Around the World in a Day*, which goes double platinum. *Purple Rain* is still going strong and wins an Oscar, three American Music Awards, and three Grammys.

1986   Prince records the album *Parade*, the soundtrack album to his second film, *Under the Cherry Moon*, which flops at the box office.

1987   Prince's state-of-the-art recording studio Paisley Park opens in Minneapolis. *Sign "☮" the Times*, a double album is released to critical acclaim. Prince also records *The Black Album* but decides not to release it.

1988   *Lovesexy* is released as a positive alternative to the *Black Album*, which by now has become a sought-after bootleg and Prince tours the United States.

1989   Prince changes managers after financial difficulties and records the soundtrack to the Tim Burton film *Batman*, which goes platinum.

1990   A new movie, *Graffiti Bridge*, tanks at the box office. Meanwhile, Prince finances a new Minneapolis nightclub called Glam Slam.

1991   Lawsuits between Prince and former manager are settled out of court; *Diamonds and Pearls*, a new album marks a commercial return for Prince after it sells 5 million copies.

1992   Prince signs a $100 million record deal with Warner Bros., who agree to become a partner on Paisley Park; the first album of the deal is titled with a symbol and sells 1 million copies.

1993   On his 35th birthday, Prince changes his name to an unpronounceable symbol that combines the signs for male and female.

1994   Paisley Park Records is dissolved, and Prince forms NPG Records. *The Black Album* and *Come* are released; an unhappy Artist Formerly Known as Prince tries to get out of his Warner Bros. contract.

1996   On Valentine's Day, the Artist Formerly Known as Prince marries Mayte Garcia and debuts a new Web site. After releasing *Chaos & Disorder*, The Artist severs ties to Warner Bros. and signs with EMI-Capitol Music Group. The first album with EMI, *Emancipation*, comes out in November.

1997   The Artist and Mayte become the parents of a baby boy, but the child dies seven days after birth from a genetic condition.

1998   Two new albums, *Crystal Ball* and *New Power Soul*, are released less than six months apart.

1999   The Artist signs with Arista records, releases *Rave Un2 the Joy Fantastic*, and performs his song "1999" on New Year's Eve.

2000   The Soul Train Music Awards name him Artist of the Decade; changes his name back to Prince in May, and ends his marriage to Mayte.

2001   Prince becomes a Jehovah's Witness; his father dies in August; marries Manuela Testolini on New Year's Eve.

2004   Prince and Beyoncé open the 46th annual Grammy Awards with a rendition of "Purple Rain." In March Prince is inducted into the Rock and Roll Hall of Fame. Soon after, he begins his first tour in six years to promote a new record, *Musicology*.

2005   He records songs as a tribute to the victims of Hurricane Katrina.

2006   In February, Prince guests on *Saturday Night Live*, his first appearance in 17 years. He releases the album *Ultimate* in August and writes "Song of the Heart" for the animated movie *Happy Feet*.

2007   Prince rocks the halftime show at Super Bowl XLI in February. During the summer he plays 21 sold out shows in London.

2008   *Indigo Night*, a live album, is released; also releases a book of poems and lyrics titled *21 Nights*.

2009   In January, Prince launches a new Web site, Lotusflow3r, and a three-album set of the same name sold exclusively at Target stores.

Albums

1978	*For You*
1979	*Prince*
1980	*Dirty Mind*
1981	*Controversy*
1982	*1999*
1984	*Purple Rain*
1985	*Around the World in a Day*
1986	*Parade*
1987	*Sign "☮" the Times*
1988	*Lovesexy*
1989	*Batman*
1990	*Graffiti Bridge*
1991	*Diamonds and Pearls*
1992	*Love Symbol*
1994	*Come*
	The Black Album
1995	*The Gold Experience*
1996	*Chaos and Disorder*
	Emancipation
1999	*Rave Un2 the Joy Fantastic*
2001	*The Rainbow Children*
2002	*One Nite Alone . . .*
2003	*Xpectation*
	N.E.W.S
2004	*Musicology*
	The Chocolate Invasion
	The Slaughterhouse
2006	*3121*
2007	*Planet Earth*
2009	*Lotusflow3r*

Films

1984	*Purple Rain*
1986	*Under the Cherry Moon*
1990	*Graffiti Bridge*

Awards

1985	Grammy Award, Best Rock Vocal Performance by a Duo or Group, for *Purple Rain* (with The Revolution)
	Grammy Award, Best R&B Song, for *I Feel For You*
	Grammy Award, Best Album of Original Score Written for a Motion Picture or Television Special, for *Purple Rain* (shared with Lisa Coleman, Wendy Melvoin, and John L. Nelson)
	Academy Award, Best Music, Original Song Score, for *Purple Rain*
	American Music Award, Favorite Soul/R&B Single, for *When Doves Cry*
	American Music Award, Favorite Soul/R&B Album, for *Purple Rain*
	American Music Award, Favorite Pop/Rock Album, for *Purple Rain*
1987	Razzie Award, Worst Actor, for *Under the Cherry Moon*
	Razzie Award, Worst Director, for *Under the Cherry Moon*
	Razzie Award, Worst Original Song , for *Love or Money* (from *Under the Cherry Moon*)
	Grammy Award, Best R&B Vocal Performance by a Duo or Group, for *Kiss* (with The Revolution)
1988	MTV Video Music Award, Best Male Video, for *U Got The Look*
	MTV Video Music Award, Best Stage Performance Video, for *U Got The Look*
1990	ASCAP Award Most Performed Songs from Motion Pictures (from movie *Batman*), for *Partyman*
	AMA Award of Achievement
1991	ASCAP Award, Most Performed Songs from Motion Pictures (from movie *Graffiti Bridge*), for *Thieves in the Temple*
1992	Soul Train Heritage Award for Career Achievement
	Brit Award, Best International Solo Artist
1993	Brit Award, Best International Solo Artist
2000	Soul Train Music Award, Artist of the Decade—Male
2004	Rock and Roll Hall of Fame Inductee
2005	Grammy Award, Best Traditional R&B Vocal Performance, for *Musicology*
	NAACP Vanguard Award
	NAACP Image Award, Outstanding Album, for *Musicology*
2006	BET Award, Best Male R&B Artist
2007	Golden Globe, Best Original Song—Motion Picture (from movie *Happy Feet*), for *The Song of the Heart*
	NAACP Image Award for Outstanding Male Artist
2008	Grammy Award, Best R&B Male Vocal Performance, for *Future Baby Mama*

acronym—word formed from the initial letters in a series of words.

androgynous—neither clearly masculine nor clearly feminine in appearance.

angst—feeling of anxiety, often including depression.

dysfunctional—abnormal or unhealthy functioning.

eclectic—selecting or choosing from various sources.

falsetto—an unnaturally or artificially high-pitched voice.

Grunge—style of rock music that incorporates elements of punk rock and heavy metal.

hieroglyph—figure or symbol with a hidden meaning.

icon—important and enduring symbol.

journeyman—any experienced, competent worker or performer.

juggernaut—any large, overpowering, force, such as a giant battleship or powerful football team.

lineage—the descendants of a common ancestor.

lucrative—profitable or moneymaking.

maestro—master in an art, especially a composer, conductor, or music teacher.

mantra—commonly repeated word or phrase.

melodious—agreeable to hear.

milestone—significant event or stage in the life, progress, or development of a person.

muse—guiding spirit; a source of inspiration.

nemesis—an opponent who is always difficult to beat or overcome.

paramour—lover or significant other.

prodigy—child or young person having extraordinary talent or ability.

prolific—producing in large quantities or with great frequency.

protégé—person who receives support and protection from an influential patron who furthers the protégé's career.

pseudonym—fake name used by an author to conceal his or her identity.

Books

Carcieri, Matthew. *Prince: A Life in Music*. Bloomington, IN: iuniverse, 2004.

Hahn, Alex. *Possessed: The Rise and Fall of Prince*. New York: Billboard Books, 2003.

Perone, James E. *The Words and Music of Prince*. Santa Barbara, California: Praeger Publishers, 2008.

Prince and Randee St. Nicholas. *21 Nights*. New York: Atria Books, 2008.

Web Sites

http://www.lotusflow3r.com

This, the latest Web site from Prince, can be fully accessed by paying a yearly fee of $77. Subscribers receive a copy of Prince's latest album, access to past videos and music, and exclusive concert footage.

http://www.prince.org

Billing itself as an "independent and unofficial . . . fan community site," this site includes a Prince-themed blog, recent news stories, and a photo gallery. Most helpful may be the Princepedia—a cyber encyclopedia of all things Purple and Princely. Best of all, membership is free!

http://new.music.yahoo.com/prince/

In recent years, the Purple One has filed lawsuits barring fan Web sites from posting his music and album art. But this Yahoo! Fan site remains live and contains a solid sampling of information on and photographs of the mysterious music man. Front and center are a modest but worthwhile selection of video clips.

PICTURE CREDITS

ABOUT THE AUTHOR

David Robson is the recipient of two playwriting fellowships from the Delaware Division of the Arts, and his plays have been performed across the country and abroad. He is also the author of several Mason Crest titles for young readers, including *Chris Rock*, *Randy Moss*, *Brian Westbrook*, and *Miley Cyrus*. David holds an M.F.A. from Goddard College, an M.S. from Saint Joseph's University, and a B.A. from Temple University. He lives with his family in Wilmington, Delaware.